ALSO BY DAVID KITCHEN

Axed Behind the Ears

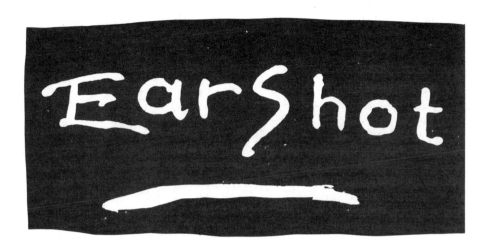

A POETRY ANTHOLOGY

EDITED BY

D A V I D K I T C H E N

HEINEMANN
EDUCATIONAL

Heinemann Educational
a division of Heinemann Educational Books Ltd
Halley Court, Jordan Hill, Oxford OX2 8EJ

OXFORD   LONDON   EDINBURGH
MADRID   ATHENS   BOLOGNA   PARIS
MELBOURNE   SYDNEY   AUCKLAND
IBADAN   NAIROBI   HARARE   GABORONE
SINGAPORE   TOKYO   PORTSMOUTH NH (USA)

ISBN 0 435 14032 9

I'd like to dedicate this book to the pupils of Howardian
High School who worked with me in all kinds of ways on
the text and especially to 1R who studied so hard and
enjoyed so much.
Equally I'd like to thank Alison who gives me the time,
the space and the love in order to be able to write.

Cover design by Caroline Alison
Photographs on pages 15, 65, 96 and 101 by Fred Davis
Printed in England by Clays Ltd, St Ives plc

CONTENTS

INTRODUCTION

This book is about getting a taste for poetry. There's every chance for that to happen because the material was chosen by hundreds of young people who know what they like and knew what their friends would like. It is also about chewing over the poetry a little and finding what is there after a second or third reading. Even more important than that, it's about how the way that one person writes can stimulate someone else to write well.

How was the selection made? Every poem was read by between fifty and one hundred young people aged from eleven to fourteen years old. If a poem produced a significant negative response, or if the most positive reaction was 'all right', then that poem was deleted. From several hundred original possibilities they produced an anthology that was some twenty poems longer than the present book. Nearly all of those poems were removed simply because they were too similar to another poem in the volume. I believe that the result is a genuinely pupil-centred selection which is also balanced and varied.

The anthology also represents a year of lessons with various classes but particularly with one class at Howardian High School. Work connected with the poems formed the core of their work in English during one year. Their excellent end-of-year results suggest that poetry, properly taught, is not only enjoyable but also a wonderful sharpener of both reading and writing.

I have not attempted to suggest work for every single poem. There should be space to browse and to read for the sheer pleasure of it. There are, however, over forty assignments and these include pages given over to reviewing and to the self-assessment of pupil's work.

The poems were chosen for their individual merits. On occasions they have been paired or clustered thematically when it appeared to be possible and appropriate. Not surprisingly the themes include school, animals, fear, food, mystery, wordplay, weather and the future. More details on where to find these poems and where to find particular types of assignments can be found in the Index on pages 109–10.

The answers to the riddles on pages 56 and 57 are snow, a river, clouds, a pavement, dew and the warmth of the sun, a promise and a blackberry. With a group defeated by the puzzling out of them, you may wish to give the answers jumbled up and ask them to attach the right answer to each riddle.

The other puzzle poem is 'Really I Did' on page 55. The answer is to move the comma from the end to the middle of each line.

How you start to work with poetry is up to you. My preference is to let pupils browse and then choose one poem to prepare for reading aloud. Other teachers I know like to start by getting some instant reactions on paper to a chosen poem and then asking partners to comment in writing on those reactions before class discussion. However you start I hope this book will help poetry come alive in a whole range of situations.

David Kitchen

I Chose This Poem Because . . . .

Much of the fun in browsing through a poetry book is choosing the poems that you like best of all.

And, just as it is with the chocolate box, different people will have different favourites. Why?

Part of the reason is that different people have different tastes.

Another part of the reason is that some people see good qualities in a poem which other people might miss.

This makes sharing our ideas and thoughts about a poem interesting and unpredictable.

A lot of people are too lazy to think about what it is that they like about a poem, but it's worth the effort.

To make it a little bit easier, here are a few questions that might help your brain tick over:

a What do you think the poem is about?
b What memories are stirred by the poem?
c What feelings does it create?
d Does the poem say something with which you agree?
e Are there especially good lines or verses?
f What is good about them?
g What is particularly sad or funny about this poem?

Remember you are sharing your enthusiasm about a poem, you are trying to get other people interested in it.

First, however, **choose your poem**.

When you have read it over two or three times, **write in rough as much as you can about your reaction to it**.

When you come to a grinding halt look at the list of questions **a** to **g**. **Look at each question to see if it helps you to add anything to what you have already written**.

When you have added all that you can, go over your rough copy.

Is there any repetition?

Are the sentences clear?

Could ideas be put into a better order?

If you are not sure about a particular part, ask a friend to read it over to see if it makes good sense to them.

When you are satisfied, write your fair copy to let others know about this poem.

Me by Me

You do piles and piles of written work, then an older person comes along and messes it up with red ink. Next day, you do another pile of work and the older person comes along again and . . . sometimes, lessons can get to look like that.

There's no point in anyone using red ink if you don't get something out of it. As much as half the red ink that gets scribbled over books never gets read. Even worse, it's very rare for someone to read over their work to see if they agree with any comments.

Instead of letting other people write about you, this is your opportunity to report on your own work.

For this to be useful, you need to have done a reasonable number of the pieces of work suggested by this book.

With a piece of rough paper handy, look back over the work you've done. Write down anything that strikes you about your work.

In particular, try to answer these questions:
- **do I agree with the teacher's comments?**
- **if I disagree, what do I disagree about?**
- **where have I done particularly good work?**
- **what weaknesses do I notice?**
- **where and how do I need to improve?**

Once you have scribbled some notes about all this, you will be almost ready to write a short report on yourself.

Before you write that report there may be one or two matters about which you are unsure or want a second opinion. Do not be afraid to ask another member of your group what they think. Usually your own opinion of your work is lower than other people's so you will probably be cheered up.

If you have time after you have written your report, take the opportunity to improve one of the pieces you were less satisfied with.

How to Eat a Poem

Don't be polite.
Bite in.
Pick it up with your fingers and lick the juice that
    may run down your chin.
It is ready and ripe now, whenever you are.

You do not need a knife or fork or spoon
or plate or napkin or tablecloth.

For there is no core
or stem
or rind
or pit
or seed
or skin
to throw away.

EVE MERRIAM

A Boy's Head

In it there is a space-ship
and a project
for doing away with piano lessons.

And there is
Noah's ark,
which shall be first.

And there is
an entirely new bird,
an entirely new hare,
an entirely new bumble-bee.

There is a river
that flows upwards.

There is a multiplication table.

There is anti-matter.

And it just cannot be trimmed.

I believe
that only what cannot be trimmed
is a head.

There is much promise
in the circumstance
that so many people have heads.

MIROSLAV HOLUB

In my Head

a Get a piece of rough paper.
Write down the first thing that comes into your head.
And the next.
And the next.   (*3 minutes maximum.*)

b Look at what you've written.
Is that typical of you?
Write down two or three things that *are* typical of you, the sort of things you think about a
lot.   (*3 minutes maximum.*)

c Now imagine you're in a warm comfortable bed; you're just dozing off, beginning to dream.
... What are you dreaming of?
Try to write a paragraph about the scene that you imagine in your head.
Read that over.
Have you got the details right?
Are any details missing?

d Change the scene.
It's a miserable night. You're trying to get to sleep but it's been one of those days when all
the things that sometimes go wrong *have* gone wrong. What are you thinking?   (*Three or
four sentences ought to be enough.*)

e Are there any things inside your head that you've not put on paper as yet? Write them down
now.   (*3 minutes maximum.*)   Then turn over the page.

In it are ways and means
Of getting dad to give me money.
Some chance!

                                        John

In it, bloodthirsty ideas pass:
Ogres, orcs and goblins at war,
Attacking the land at night.

                                        Dinesh

In it are plans for the
Largest sweetest chocolate eclair,
A classroom sprayed pink
And lessons standing on your head.

                                        Dina

3

f Now the fun starts.

You're going to find out what other people think is inside your head. Whatever they say, write it down in rough, even if you disagree. Ask your friends, your family, perhaps even a teacher or two. Try to get at least five or six opinions.

g You should now have plenty of material to write about the inside of your head, but how will you organise it?

Will you use some or all of it?

Which part will you use first?

Which part makes a good ending?

Which parts contrast well with each other?

Mark the order on your rough copy and begin to make an improved copy.

h What you have now got is unlikely to be perfect but it should show traces of a pattern.

Show it to a friend.

Ask them about the order.

Does it work?

Has anything important been left out?

Make any changes you think will improve it and write your final version.

Me

My mum is on a diet,
My dad is on the booze,
My gran's out playing Bingo
And she was born to lose.

My brother's stripped his motorbike
Although it's bound to rain.
My sister's playing Elton John
Over and over again.

What a dim old family!
What a dreary lot!
Sometimes I think that I'm the only
Superstar they've got.

KIT WRIGHT

You!

You!
Your head is like a hollow drum.
You!
Your eyes are like balls of flame.
You!
Your ears are like fans for blowing fire.
You!
Your nostril is like a mouse's hole.
You!
Your mouth is like a lump of mud.
You!
Your hands are like drum-sticks.
You!
Your belly is like a pot of bad water.
You!
Your legs are like wooden posts.
You!
Your backside is like a mountain-top.

from the IGBO PEOPLE OF NIGERIA

And What About You?

How would you describe your eyes, your ears, your stomach?
How would you describe your brain, your mouth, your legs?
What about your clothes, your hair, your voice?
And what about your character, your personality?
What could you say about your reliability?
What are you like with money?
Do you work hard?
What are you like with other people's secrets?
What are you like for turning up on time?

Saying what something is like is never easy but see what you can come up with.

Growing Up

I know a lad called Billy
Who goes along with me
He plays this game
Where he uses my name
And makes people think that he's me.

Don't ever mess with Billy
He's a vicious sort of bloke
He'll give you a clout
For saying nowt
And thump you for a joke.

My family can't stand Billy
Can't bear him around the place
He won't eat his food
He's always rude
And wears scowls all over his face.

No one can ever break Billy
He's got this look in his eye
That seems to say
You can whale me all day
But you'll not make Billy cry.

He has a crazy face has Billy
Eyes that look but can't see
A mouth like a latch
Ears that don't match
And a space where his brains should be.

Mad Billy left one morning
Crept away without being seen
Left his body for me
That fits perfectly
And a calm where his madness had been.

GARETH OWEN

A Black Man's Song

I looked in the mirror.
What did I see?
Not black not white,
but me, only me.

        Coal black face
        with big bright eyes
        and lily white teeth
        that's lil old me.

Yes I looked in the mirror.
What did I see?
I saw a fella
who's dear to me.

        Short broad nose,
        full thick lips
        and black kinky hair;
        man that's me.

Oh I looked in the mirror.
What did I see?
I saw a fella
as cute as can be,

        that must be me.

If you look
in the mirror,
what will you see?

        You may see black,
        you may see white;
        but you won't see me,
        no siree not me.

JIMI RAND

Descriptive Writing

Before you turn over the page to read 'Catalogue' and 'The Tom-Cat', here are some ideas to think about.

Most people find it is much easier to say what happened than to say what the scene looked like at the moment something happened. If you want to check the truth of that, ask any police officer how bad most people are at giving eye witness descriptions.

There is no easy way to make your descriptive writing as good as your story-telling, but you can get better.

One way to improve is to watch the everyday scenes that you take for granted more carefully.

Next time you're in the High Street, look up so that you can take in the whole of the buildings you're looking at and not just the ground floor. You'll be surprised at the things you've missed even though you've walked down the street hundreds of times.

Next time you're standing around, waiting for someone, look at the people who are passing. How would you describe their faces? What clothes are they wearing?

Another way to improve your powers of description is to learn from other people. On the following pages you can read descriptions of cats by Rosalie Moore and Don Marquis. The poems are very different but both are attempting to capture something about the essence of cats in words. Both writers are doing more than writing down the facts about cats. They're encouraging you to use your imagination to conjure up your own picture. If you want to write better: read, enjoy your reading and don't hurry.

A third way to help descriptive writing is not to write too much. Concentrating on getting a very few words absolutely right can be much better practice than writing ten pages that you don't think about as you're scribbling it down. That's why you'll have a number of opportunities in this book to write very short descriptions. One of them, in fact, comes up straight after the two poems on cats.

Catalogue

Cats sleep fat and walk thin.
Cats, when they sleep, slump.
When they wake, stretch and begin
Over, pulling their ribs in.
Cats walk thin.

Cats wait in a lump.
Jump in a streak.
Cats, when they jump are sleek
As a grape slipping through its skin –
They have technique.
Oh, cats don't creak
They sneak.

Cats sleep fat.
They spread out comfort underneath them
Like a good mat.
As if they picked the place.
And then sat.
You walk around one
As if he were the city hall
After that

If Male
A cat is apt to sing on a major scale.
This concert is for everybody, this
Is wholesale.
For a baton, he wields a tail.
(He is also found
When happy, to resound
With an enclosed and private sound.)

A cat condenses.
He pulls his tail to go under bridges.
And himself to go under fences.
Cats fit
In any size box or kit.
And if a large pumpkin grew under one,
He could arch over it.

When everybody else is just ready to go out,
The cat is just ready to come in.
He's not where he's been.
Cats sleep fat and walk thin.

ROSALIE MOORE

The Tom-Cat

At midnight in the alley
A Tom-cat comes to wail,
And he chants the hate of a million years
As he swings his snaky tail.

Malevolent, bony, brindled,
Tiger and devil and bard,
His eyes are coals from the middle of Hell
And his heart is black and hard.

He twists and crouches and capers
And bares his curved sharp claws,
And he sings to the stars of the jungle nights,
Ere cities were, or laws.

Beasts from a world primeval,
He and his leaping clan,
When the blotched red moon lears over the roofs,
Give voice to their scorn of man.

He will lie on a rug tomorrow
And lick his silky fur,
And veil the brute in his yellow eyes
And play he's tame, and purr.

But at midnight in the alley
He will crouch again and wail,
And beat the time for his demon's song,
With the swing of his demon's tail.

DON MARQUIS

Describing Cats

Fourteen words.
That's all you need to do this so be careful about the ones you choose.
Arrange the words in four lines like this:

_____	_____	_____	_____
_____	_____	_____	
_____	_____	_____	_____
_____	_____	_____	

Every word should add something to your description.
Not one word should be wasted.

For your first attempt at this, use words from the two poems on cats. You can change the form of the words if you like: 'sleep', for example, could be changed to 'sleeping'. Remember, fourteen words. None wasted.

Once you're satisfied with that, try and find words of your own to describe cats and put them into another four lines.

Bad Dog

All day long, Bones hasn't been seen
– But now he comes slinking home
Smelling of ditches and streams
And pastures and pinewoods and loam
And tries to crawl under my bed.
His coat is caked with mud,
And one of his ears drips blood.
Nobody knows where he's been.

'Who did it?' they ask him, 'who . . .?
He'll have to be bathed . . the sinner . . .
Pack him off to his basket . . .
You *bad dog*, you'll get no dinner . . .'
And he cowers, and rolls an eye.
Tomorrow, I *won't* let him go –
But he licks my hand, and then – oh,
How I wish that I had been too.

BRIAN LEE

Old Dog

Toward the last in the morning she could not
get up, even when I rattled her pan.
I helped her into the yard, but she stumbled
and fell. I knew it was time.

The last night a mist drifted over the fields;
in the morning she would not raise her head –
the far, clear mountains we had walked
surged back to mind.

We looked a slow bargain: our days together
were the ones we already had.
I gave her something the vet had given,
and patted her still, a good last friend.

WILLIAM STAFFORD

My Gerbil

Once I had a gerbil –
Bought me by my Dad
I used to watch it in its cage,
Running round like mad
Or sleeping in a corner
Nesting in a hole
Made of shavings, bits of wool
And chewed up toilet roll.

I kept it in the kitchen
In the cage my cousin made.
It flicked all bits out on the floor
Mum grumbled – but it stayed.
I fed it; gave it water;
Was going to buy a wheel.
I used to take it out sometimes –
To stroke. I liked the feel –
All soft, with needle eyes,
A little throbbing chest.
I'd had a bird, a hamster too:
The gerbil I liked best.

I came downstairs one morning.
I always came down first.
In the cage there was no movement.

At once I knew the worst.
He lay there in the corner.
He'd never once been ill –
But now, fur frozen, spiky,
No throbbing, eye quite still.

I tell you – I just stood there
And quietly cried and cried,
And, when my Mum and Dad came down,
I said, 'My gerbil's died.'

And still I kept on crying,
Cried all the way to school,
But soon stopped when I got there
They'd all call me a fool.

I dawdled home that evening.
There, waiting, was my mother.
Said: 'Would you like another one?'
But I'll never want another.

JOHN KITCHING

Execution

It was a pig's head in a window that started it,
An apple in its jaws, eyes decently lidded,
Flesh like carved tallow.
I was glad the eyes were closed over the accusation,
For I saw with a shiver another Tom,
My father's pig when I was seven.
We were all there in the cramped theatre
Of the little yard,
The girls in curlers and fluffy slippers,
The women's hand restless in hessian aprons,
Children wide-eyed and silent,
And the men gruff and wary . . .
You can't be ceremonious with jaws
That can crunch an ankle.
Tom, with what looked like contempt in those tiny eyes
Plodded with a certain porcine dignity
To execution.

They tripped his legs
And slammed a plank across his head.
Tied up his feet and six fat men
Sprawled on his struggling body.
Little Mr Walker,
Eighty, with sagging knees,
A kindly, white-haired chapel man
Who paid his pew-rent,
Balanced his frightful Monday morning knife,
And picked his way without mercy through the squeals,
Felt with a surgeon's fingers at the throat,
Paused and then gently pressed
Till the squeals gurgled in a gush of red
Over the blue-brown paving of the yard.
The bound feet kicked and kicked and twitched,
And the frail little chapel man wiped his knife
Thoughtfully,
Declined a cup of tea,
Shuffled daintily through the blood
And went for breakfast.

We gaped in horror as he clicked the gate.
Fingered our lips,
And tried uneasily to hide
The knife in every hand.

GREGORY HARRISON

Thinking it over

a Where does the writer see a pig's head?
b What does it remind him of?
c Why does Gregory Harrison describe the family's backyard as a 'theatre'?
d How old is Mr Walker?
e What do we learn about Mr Walker's appearance?
f What word is used to describe Mr Walker's character?
g What do you think about Mr Walker as an executioner?
h Why do you think Gregory Harrison chose to write about this memory of his?

Please Will You Take Your Children Home Before I Do Them In

Please will you take your children home
Before I do them in?
I kissed your little son
As he came posturing within.
I took his little jacket
And removed his little hat
But now the visit's over
So push off you little brat.

And don't think for a moment
That I didn't understand
How the hatchet he was waving
In his grotty little hand
Broke my china teapot
That I've always held so dear –
But would you mind removing him
Before I smack his ear?

Of course I wan't angry
As I shovelled up the dregs,
I'm only glad the teabags
Didn't scald his little legs.
I'm glad he liked my chocolate cake
I couldn't help but laugh
As he rubbed it in the carpet ...
Would he like the other half?

He guzzled all the orange
And he guzzled all the Coke –
The only thing that kept me sane
Was hoping he might choke.
And then he had a mishap,
Well, I couldn't bear to look,
Do something for your Auntie little sunshine ...
Sling your hook.

He's been playing in the garden
And he's throttled all the flowers,
Give the lad a marlinspike
He'll sit out there for hours.
I've gathered my insecticides
And marked them with their name
And put them up where children
Couldn't reach them. That's a shame.

Still he must have liked my dog
Because he choked her half to death,
She'll go out for another game
Once she's caught her breath.
He rode her round the garden
And he lashed her with his rope
She's never bitten anyone
But still, we live in hope.

He's kicked the TV now!
I like to see it getting booted
Kick it one more time son
You might get electrocuted!
Yes, turn up the volume,
Twist the knobs, me little treasure
And when the programme's over
There's the door. It's been a pleasure.

PAM AYRES

Why?

Why are the leaves always green, Dad?
Why are there thorns on a rose?
Why do you want my neck clean, Dad?
Why do hairs grow from your nose?

Why can dogs hear what we can't, Dad?
Why has the engine just stalled?
Why are you rude about Aunt, Dad?
Why are you going all bald?

Why is Mum taller than you, Dad?
Why can't the dog stand the cat?
Why's Grandma got a moustache, Dad?
Why are you growing more fat?

Why don't you answer my questions?
You used to; you don't any more.
Why? Tell me why. Tell me why, Dad?
Do you think I am being a bore?

JOHN KITCHING

Why?

Why do you always sit in that chair, dad?
Because I like this chair.
Why haven't you got a car dad?
Because they cost too much money.
Why don't you read dad?
Because I don't like reading.
Why don't you write dad?
Because I don't have anyone to write to.
Why did you marry mum, dad?
Because she was pretty.
Why isn't she now, dad?
She is but she did have you.

Craig

Questions

Is that how it is in your house?
Who do you nag with questions?
  Write a conversation between you and your father/mother/elder sister/hamster in which you keep asking questions just like the child does in John Kitching's poem.

23

The Man in the Wilderness

The Man in the Wilderness asked of me
'How many blackberries grow in the sea?'
I answered him as I thought good,
'As many red herrings as grow in the wood.'

The Man in the Wilderness asked my why
His hen could swim, and his pig could fly.
I answered him briskly as I thought best,
'Because they were born in a cuckoo's nest.'

The man in the Wilderness asked me to tell
The sands in the sea and I counted them well.
Says he with a grin, 'And not one more?'
I answered him bravely, 'You go and make sure!'

ANON

Intelligence Test

'What do you use your eyes for?'
The white-coated man enquired.
'I use my eyes for looking,'
Said Toby, '– unless I'm tired.'

'I see. And then you close them,'
Observed the white-coated man.
'Well done. A very good answer.
Let's try another one.

'What is your nose designed for?
What use is the thing to you?'
'I use my nose for smelling,'
Said Toby, 'Don't you, too?'

'I do indeed,' said the expert,
'That's what the thing is for.
Now I've another question to ask you,
Then there won't be any more.

'What are your ears intended for?
Those things at each side of your head?
Come on – don't be shy – I'm sure you can say.'
'For washing behind,' Toby said.

VERNON SCANNELL

Teachers – the Inside Story

Rodge said,
'Teachers – they want it all ways –
You're jumping up and down on a chair
or something
and they grab hold of you and say,
'Would you do that sort of thing in your own home?'

So you say, 'No'
And they say,
'Well don't do it here then.'

But if you say, 'Yes, I do it at home'
they say,
'Well, we don't want that sort of thing
going on here
thank you very much.'

'Teachers – they get you all ways,'
Rodge said.

MICHAEL ROSEN

A Guide to Teachertalk

Life might be a lot more fun, at times, if teachers said what they were thinking rather than wrapping everything up in long polite phrases.

Perhaps, in fact, it it time to provide a guide to those polite phrases and what they mean.

Below are a few examples just to get you started:

Could put more effort into his work.

means Hasn't brought a pen for over six months.

Needs clear and firm guidance

means Should be buried alive.

Has not quite adjusted to the social opportunities provided by the school.

means Spent five hours locked in a toilet cubicle yesterday refusing to talk to anyone.

Our School

I go to Weld Park Primary,
It's near the Underpass
And five blocks past the Cemetery
And two roads past the Gas
Works with the big tower that smells so bad
   me and me mates put our hankies over our
      faces and pretend we're being attacked
         by poison gas . . . and that.

There's this playground with lines for rounders,
And cricket stumps chalked on the wall,
And kids with their coats for goalposts
Booting a tennis ball
Around all over the place and shoutin' and arguin'
   about offside and they always kick it over
      the garden wall next door and she
         goes potty and tells our head teacher
         and he gets right ratty with
            everybody and stops us playin'
            football . . .
              . . . and everything.

We have this rule at our school
You've to wait till the whistle blows
And you can't go in till you hear it
Not even if it snows
And your wellies get filled with water and your socks
   go all soggy and start slipping down your legs
      and your hands get so cold they go all
         crumpled and you can't undo
         the buttons of your mac when
          you do get inside . . .
          .. it's true.

The best thing is our classroom.
When it's fine you can see right far,
Past the Catholic Cathedral
Right to the Morris Car
Works where me Dad works as a fitter and sets off
    right early every morning in those overalls
        with his snap in his sandwich box and
            a flask of tea and always moanin'
                about the money ... honest.

In Hall we pray for brotherly love
And sing hymns that are ever so long
And the Head shouts at Linda Nutter
Who's always doing wrong.
She can't keep out of trouble because
    she's always talkin'
        she can't stop our teacher says she
            must have been injected with
                a gramophone needle she talks
                    so much and
    that made me laugh once
                once
        not any more though I've heard it
            too often ... teachers!

Loving your enemy sounds all right
Until you open your eyes
And you're standing next to Nolan
Who's always telling lies
About me and getting me into trouble and about
    three times a week I fight him after school
        It's like a habit I've got
            but I can't love him even though
                I screw my eyes up real hard and try like
                    mad, but if it wasn't him it
                        would be somebody else
                        I mean
                    You've got to have enemies ...
                        ... haven't you?

We sing 'O to be a pilgrim'
And think about God and heaven
And we're told the football team lost
By thirteen goals to seven
But that's not bad because St Xavier's don't half have
    big lads in their team and last time we played
        they beat us eighteen one and this time
            we got seven goals ...
                ... didn't we?

Then we have our lessons,
We have Science and English and Maths,
Except on Wednesday morning
When our class goes to the baths
And it's not half cold and Peter Bradberry's
   fingers went all wrinkled and blue last week
     and I said, 'You're goin' to die, man'
       but he pushed me under the water and I had to
         hold my breath for fifteen minutes.
           But he's still alive though . . .
             . . . he is.

Friday's my favourite day though,
We have Art all afternoon
And I never care what happens
Cos I know it's home-time soon
And I'm free for two whole days but I think
   sometimes it wouldn't be half so good
     having this weekend if we didn't have five
       days
         of
           school
             in
               between –

Would it?

                GARETH OWEN

Thinking it over

a Give each of the nine verses of 'Our School' a title of its own which describes generally what that verse is about.

b Look carefully at the first verse. What subject does it start with and how does it end?

c Look at the third verse and see if you can make the same sort of division into two subjects.

d At what point in the third verse would you divide it into two?

e What happens to the layout of the lines in the verse at that point?

f See if you can divide each of the verses into two parts.

g In what way is the style of writing in the second part of each verse different from the writing in the first part?

h Look back at the third verse again and at the last two words. What is the point of those words?

i Are there similar last words in every verse?

j See if you can write just one verse about your last school using the same structure as Gareth Owen has used in his poem.

What, Miss?

Homework?
Did we have homework?

You was away on Monday, miss,
So we thought you'd be away today.

I've done it, miss,
But I've left my book up my nan's.

I lent my book to Darren
And he's away today.

I've got my book, miss,
But I did the work on paper
And I think I left it at home.

My baby sister
Got hold of all my books
And was sick on them.

I thought I had a dental appointment
This morning, miss,
But it's this afternoon
So I've got the books for this afternoon
When I'll be at the dentist
But I haven't got this morning's books
Because I thought I wan't here.

I had a brain relapse, miss.

DAVID KITCHEN

Excuses

Now you don't often have an opportunity to tell a decent-sized lie and get away with it. This is your chance.

Imagine that you arrive at school on Monday morning without your English book which, of course, has your homework in it.

Write an explanation of how you come to be without your homework. Your story, like most excuses, should be long and complicated . . . and probably untrue.

The School Caretaker

In the corner of the playground
Down dark and slimy stairs,
Lived a Monster with a big nose
Full of curly hairs.

He had a bunch of keyrings
Carved out of little boys,
He confiscated comics
And all our favourite toys.

He wore a greasy uniform,
Looked like an undertaker,
More scary than a horror film,
He was the school caretaker.

I left the school some years ago;
Saw him again the other day.
He looked rather sad and old
Shuffling on his way.

It's funny when you grow up
How grown-ups start growing down,
And the snarls upon their faces
Are no more than a frown.

In the corner of the playground
Down dark and slimy stairs.
Sits a lonely little man
With a nose full of curly hairs.

BRIAN PATTEN

The other side

What do you imagine that the school caretaker thinks of you?

What goes through his head as he walks around the school after you've gone home?

What work does he do when the school is empty?

Either
Write a piece based on the thoughts of a school caretaker as he goes around one evening. (You may find this easier if you write it as if you were the school caretaker.)

Or
Imagine you stay very late one night and you're the last person left on the premises except for the caretaker. Because you are the last two, you get chatting and he tells you a bit about his life and his job . . .

The Ballad of Darren Cullen

This is the case of Darren Cullen
    (Blue eyes, six foot three),
His Dad, his teacher (Mrs Spence)
    And his headmaster (me).

Big Darren's Daddy picked him up
    When the lad was two foot tall
And swung him by the ankles hard
    Against the bedroom wall.

Young Darren leaned around the back
    Of the Star and Garter Inn
While his Daddy bought his Auntie Chris
    Her seventh double gin.

And when the boy was five foot tall
    They caught him in Grigson's Yard
Driving a forklift truck around
    The piles of packing card.

Down by the gloomiest canal
    In the gloomiest weather
Darren reached the start of his youth
    And the end of his short tether.

His teacher, knowing the school was built
    For her own peace and quiet,
Gently tickled in him one day
    His tendency to riot.

'Nobody loves you Darren Cullen
    And I will tell you why . . .'
She said, and found no going on
    For the death in Darren's eye.

He's taken from a new display
    Of farming implements
A horse mane docker, and it's aimed
    At Mrs Muriel Spence.

The headmaster's praying suddenly
    And his lunge is rather tardy –
The thing is sticking neatly out
    Of Mrs Spence's cardy.

After a vivid afternoon
    They found out what you've guessed –
The horse mane docker hardly got
    Beyond Mu Spence's vest.

Thank God, we said. Darren was carted
    Off to special school
For scaring a teacher witless with
    An agricultural tool.

These days the lad is six foot three
    And he takes his revenge on all
His women nightly, and the little boy
    That he bangs on the bedroom wall.

FRED SEDGWICK

Two Old Black Men on a Leicester Square Park Bench

What do you dream of you
old black men sitting
on park benches staunchly
wrapped up in scarves
and coats of silence
eyes far away from the cold
grey and strutting
pigeon
ashy fingers trembling
(though it's said that the old
hardly ever feel the cold)

do you dream revolutions
you could have forged
or mourn
some sunfull woman you
might have known a
hibiscus flower
ghost memories of desire

O it's easy
to rainbow the past
after all the letters from
home spoke of hardships

and the sun was traded long ago

GRACE NICHOLS

The Double Picture

There are always two pictures of a person. The first you can be fairly sure about because it's the outside picture. If a woman is wearing a green raincoat and two people see her, then any disagreement is likely to be limited to what shade of green you would call the raincoat. If the woman has a distant gaze and smiles faintly, then the same two people may be set wondering about the second picture: that is, the inside look, the picture of what is going on in the mind. Two people can discuss that forever and still not be certain.

Notice how Grace Nichols in her poem describes what the two old men look like, but also spends as much time imagining what is going on in their heads.

See if you can write a piece where you not only describe what someone looks like but also what he or she is thinking.

Where do you find someone like that? Bus stops are one good place. Shopping centres are another. Simply walking to and from school you will see people who have lives, dreams, memories and fears that are unknown to you.

Watching the world go by you only see the one picture. See if you can imagine the inside look of someone as well.

He stood there, cigar in his mouth,
Holding his newspaper.
Massive eye bags drooping down his face.
His skin was well tanned like a ripe kiwi-fruit,
Wrinkled and very weather-beaten.
An ugly scar ran down his nose,
Finishing at his immensely large nostrils.
His eyes looked into nowhere,
Like the eyes of a zombie.
What he is thinking about is a mystery.
Might it be his lonesome voyage around the world,
Or going home to find his wife gone?
Maybe losing his only son in a car crash in which he was drunk,
Or losing his house and all his money in a game of poker last night?
Maybe he's forseen the end of the world?
His local pub being shut down seems a more likely reason to me.

Dipesh

Palm Tree King

Because I come from the West Indies
certain people in England seem to think
I is a expert on palm trees

So not wanting to sever dis link
with me native roots (know what ah mean?)
or to disappoint dese culture vulture
I does smile cool as seabreeze

and say to dem
which specimen
you interested in
cause you talking
to the right man
I is palm tree king
I know palm tree history
like de palm o me hand
In fact me navel string
bury under a palm tree

If you think de queen could wave
you ain't see nothing yet
till you see the Roystonea Regia
– that is the royal palm –
with she crown of leaves
waving calm-calm
over the blue Caribbean carpet
nearly 100 feet of royal highness

But let we get down to business
Tell me what you want to know
How tall a palm tree does grow?
What is the biggest coconut I ever see?
What is the average length of the leaf?

Don't expect me to be brief
cause palm tree history
is a long-long story

Anyway why you so interested
in length and circumference?
That kind of talk so ordinary
That don't touch the essence
of palm tree mystery
That is no challenge
to a palm tree historian like me

If you insist on statistics
why you don't pose a question
with some mathematical profundity?

Ask me something more tricky
like if a American tourist with a camera
take 9 minutes to climb a coconut tree
how long a English tourist without a camera
would take to climb the same coconut tree?

That is problem pardner
Now ah coming harder

If 6 straw hat
and half a dozen bikini
multiply by the same number of coconut tree
equal one postcard
how many square miles of straw hat
you need to make a tourist industry?

That is problem pardner
Find the solution
and you got a revolution

But before you say anything
let I palm tree king
give you dis warning
Ah want de answer in metric
it kind of rhyme with tropic
Besides it sound more exotic

JOHN AGARD

Do you fancy yourself as an expert?
Then turn over.

Expertise

What do you fancy being an expert on?
- – the thought process of cats?
- – the marks on the classroom floor?
- – the life and times of a snail?

You might like to write a short guide to a place you know or the history of your area.

There is only one rule. What you say must sound as convincing as possible but it should be complete and utter nonsense.

Today my subject is the humming bird. Whilst this creature is famous for its humming, it is not because it has forgotten the words. The humming bird sings every word very clearly but it does it so fast and at such a high pitch that, to our ears, it sounds like humming.

Its elongated beak comes from poking not only into flowers but also other bird's business. Over the years this shape has gradually . . . . . .

Katy

Someone Stole the   .

While I was taking a short   -nap
   someone stole the   ,
I should have spun round like a   herine wheel
   when someone stole the   .
But I was too slow to   ch them,
   when someone stole the   .

Now the   amaran can't float,
   because someone stole the   .
And the   erpillar can't crawl,
   because someone stole the   .
And the   aract can't fall,
   because someone stole the   .

It was not me and it was not you
   but it is   egorically true,
And if you were to ask me
   I'd say it was a   astrophe
That someone's stolen the   .

BRIAN PATTEN

Words in Space

They decided to abolish the words:
to sit
to stand
and to lie
and the word
to float will replace them.

So people now say:
float up straight when I'm talking to you
let sleeping dogs float
let's float down and have a chat about it.

People who don't like cabbage say,
I can't float cabbage
and they watch telly
in the floating-room.

Is there anyone who doesn't
underfloat what I'm saying?

MICHAEL ROSEN

I must burn . . .

Michael Rosen's poem shows you the strange results of changing just two or three words in the language.

Let's see what are the effects of removing a word from the language and replacing it with another word.

Suppose we replaced the word 'get' in the next two sentences.

"I must get my brother's birthday present this week."
she said.
"Get it now," said her father.

What word might replace 'get'? Burn? See what happens when you replace 'get' with 'burn'.

"I must burn my brother's birthday present this week,"
she said.
"Burn it now," said her father.

The best words to remove from the language are ordinary ones. Try writing two or three sentences in which one of these words keeps occurring.

form · catch · spot · pass · carry · sell · back · front
way · wear · fire · make · over · under · out ·
        in · strong

Now write out the sentences leaving gaps for the word you are removing.

Choose a word to replace the one you have removed.

By this time you should be able to see the possibilities for changing words around.

See if you can put your ideas together in a piece like Michael Rosen's. If you're not sure how to start, you could begin like this:

> On the planet, Mercury
> They abolished the words ..... and .....
> And replaced them with ..... and .....
> Now ...

The Teacher

Mr Grind is very kind
He goes to church on Sunday,
He prays to God to give him strength
to belt the kids on Monday.

ANON

Manners

I eat my peas with honey
I've done it all my life
It makes the peas taste funny
But it keeps 'em on the knife!

ANON

Doctor Bell

Doctor Bell fell down the well
And broke his collar-bone.
Doctors should attend the sick
And leave the well alone.

ANON

Mary Had . . .

Mary had a little lamb,
She ate it with mint sauce,
And everywhere that Mary went
The lamb went too, of course.

ANON

Can *you* create a humorous picture in only four lines? See what you can manage.

Limericks

There was a young lady from Ickenham,
Who took a bus ride down to Twickenham.
She drank so much gin,
Her stomach caved in,
So she took off her boots and was sick in 'em.

A careless old man from Blackheath,
Sat down on his set of false teeth.
He said, in his pain,
'I've done it again,
I have bitten myself underneath.'

There was a young lady of Lynn,
Who was quite uncommonly thin.
So when she was made,
To drink lemonade,
She slipped through the straw and fell in.

There was a young farmer of Leeds,
Who swallowed six packets of seeds.
It soon came to pass,
He was covered with grass,
And couldn't sit down for the weeds.

Gust Becos I Cud Not Spel

Gust becos I cud not spel
It did not mean I was daft
When the boys in school red my riting
Some of them laffed

But now I am the dictater
They have to rite like me
Utherwise they cannot pas
Ther GCSE

Some of the girls wer ok
But those who laffed a lot
Have al bean rownded up
And hav recintly bean shot

The teecher who corrected my speling
As not been shot at al
But four the last fifteen howers
As bean standing up against a wal

He has to stand ther until he can spel
Figgymisgrugifooniyn the rite way
I think he will stand ther forever
I just inventid it today

BRIAN PATTEN

Definitions

Someone has to invent the new words in our language and there is no reason why it should not be you.

First of all, though, what about 'Figgymisgrugifooniyn'? Decide what you think that word means.

After a few minutes, listen to each other's definitions of the word and decide which is best.

Then see what words you can create yourself.

(A dictionary will show you a variety of ways in which the meanings of words are set out.)

skrinkle (*v.i.*) to screw one's face up so that it looks smaller than it really is.

bluggit (*n.*) a soggy white pudding still served in school canteens in certain areas of the country.

Rods Poem

Hiyamac.
Lobuddy.
Binearlong?
Cuplours.
Ketchanenny?
Goddafew.
Kindarthay?
Bassencarp.
Enysizetoum?
Cuplapowns.
Hittinard?
Sordalite.
Wahchoozin?
Maggitsenwurms.
Fishanonaboddum?
Rydonnaboddum.
Igoddago.
Tubad.
Seeyaround.
Yeatakideezy.
Guluk.

ANON

What on earth is going on here?

Can you make any sense of it?

Really I Did

I saw a monkey making bread,
I saw a girl composed of thread,
I saw a towel one acre square,
I saw a meadow in the air,
I saw a rocket walk a mile,
I saw a pony make a file,
I saw a blacksmith in a box,
I saw an orange kill an ox,
I saw a butcher made of steel,
I saw a penknife dance a reel,
I saw a sailor twelve feet high,
I saw a ladder in a pie,
I saw an apple fly away,
I saw a sparrow making hay,
I saw a farmer and he says too
That these strange things were all quite true.

ANON

This nonsense poem becomes quite sensible when you make certain changes to the punctuation. Can you see what changes are needed?

Guess Me

White as snow and snow it isn't,
Green as grass and grass it isn't,
Red as blood and blood it isn't,
Black as tar and tar it isn't.

White sheep on a blue hill:
The wind stops, you stand still.
The wind blows, you leave slow.
White sheep, where do you go?

I washed my face in water
That had neither rained nor run,
I dried my face on a towel
That was not woven or spun.

White bird, featherless,
Floats through the air.
Trees stretch their arms,
The bird settles there.

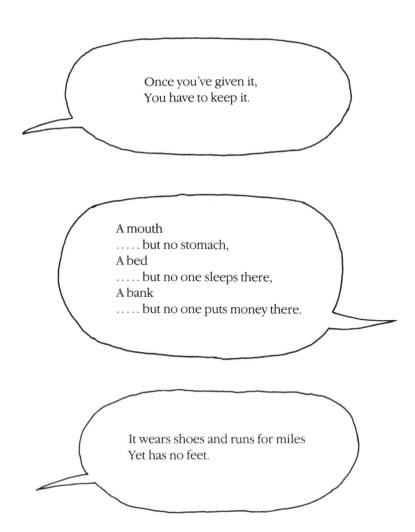

Once you've given it,
You have to keep it.

A mouth
. . . . . but no stomach,
A bed
. . . . . but no one sleeps there,
A bank
. . . . . but no one puts money there.

It wears shoes and runs for miles
Yet has no feet.

More riddles

A riddle is no more than a mysterious description of something which may well be quite ordinary.

See if you can write a description of one of the following which makes t sound puzzling or strange:

A baby   A car

Computer games   Football   A microwave oven

Television   Radio   A dentist's surgery

Christmas   Cricket

Crowds on a beach

Acrostic Poems

SWEET DREAMS

Carefully prepared
Hypoallergenic
Organically grown
Carob coated
Oat enriched
Lactose, preservative and colouring free
Approved by the vegetarian society
Tofu flavoured
Eats

MESSAGE ON THE TABLE

Your dinner is in the
Oven because I'm taking
Uncle
Jack
Up to your grandmother's.
She hasn't seen him in years.
There's also extra sauce in
A pan on the stove. It needs
To be warmed through
Even if you get in on time for once.
Wash up and
Open a can of something if you're still
Ravenous. Although you
May not be if you work out my
Secret.

Glenys,
Every moment
That I am away from you seems
Like an eternity
Only the heavy demands of business
Separate me from my one
True love.

SCHOOL REPORT

Name	James Ricott**i**
English:	Very well rea**d**
Maths:	Should do wel**l**
Art:	Another good grad**e**
History:	His project was super**b**
French:	Hard worke**r**
Science:	Deserves an **A**
Geography:	Always does his bes**t**

Everything is not always what it seems to be

We get so used to reading across that we never bother to read down the page.
An acrostic is usually formed by the first (or last) letter of each line.
For centuries this method has been used to carry secret messages.
What do you find hidden in these poems?

See if you can hide a message in an acrostic poem of your own.
The greater the difference between that you appear to be saying and what the acrostic says the better.

Lurker

The old man lurked behind a tree.
School was over, I was free.
I ran, jumped, shouted 'Cheerio'
And found some pebbles to kick and throw.
    The old man lurked behind a tree.
I went to the park to chase the birds.
I chased them all, well at least two thirds.
I went on the slide. I had a swing.
And then I stopped. I'd done everything.
    The old man lurked behind a tree.

I started for home. It was time for tea.
And my favourite programme on T.V.
I was hungry now. My tummy rumbled.
I kicked a stone. And then I stumbled.
    The old man lurked behind a tree.
'Do you want a sweet?' he said, soft and mild.
He held it out. I paused. He smiled.
Not a sound. It was getting late.
I was the fish. The sweet was the bait.
    The old man lurked behind the tree.

'Here have a sweet. Come on. It's free.'
And then I minded what Mother had said:
'If a stranger stops you, just keep your head.
If it's a man, say, "You're not my Dad."
He'll understand, if he's O.K.
In any case, just run away.'

So I kept my head. In fact, I shook it.
And that tempting sweet, I never took it.
'You're not my Dad!' I said. 'No way!'
And then I turned and ran away.
I looked back twice and I could see
    The old man still lurking behind the tree.

GEOFFREY SUMMERFIELD

Ess'ole

I always liked my grand-dad's house,
With the white fungus in the cellar,
Narrow winding stairs up to the attic,
And the amazing maze of kitchens,
Corridors, sculleries, the sheds.

Until, one day, I cheeked him to his face.
He said quite simply, 'Put the dog out, lad.'
But I was busy exploring a drawer
And said, 'Put it out yourself.'

A moment of shocked silence hung in the air,
And then the old man roared.
He coughed and spluttered, staggered,
And grabbed me by the neck.
His horny nails bit into my flesh.
'Any more lip from you, my lad,
And I'll chuck you into th'ess'ole.'

Meaning the hole for ash beneath the fire,
A hole that glowed bright red like hell,
And seemed to breathe in every draught.

For months, whenever I was bored on rainy days,
And Mother said, 'Go and see your granddad,'
Suddenly, as if by magic, I'd find lots of things to
     do
So that I needn't face the jaws of hell.

GEOFFREY SUMMERFIELD

Coming Home

It's not really scary
when you come in the house
and nobody's there

    it's just

that the chairs seem to
stare
and the room looks so big and
the deep sounds of quiet
make a buzz in your ears

    and

Mum'll be back soon
it's really all right
the teapot's all ready
I'm not at all frightened
I'll switch on the TV
but not for a minute

I'll just sit here
I don't want to move from the chair
and it's not really scary
I'm not at all frightened
and only a *Baby* would start to believe
that something invisible's
sitting behind

I'll look in a minute
Yes, that's what I'll do
in a minute I'll look

I'll just sit here
and soon I'll switch on
the TV
in a minute or two
it's only a box – after all
just a box and I know that
it can't really whisper
those horrible things
when it isn't switched on

    cos

I'm old enough now
Yes, I'm old enough now and
I don't really mind
No, I don't really mind

    cos

    it's only till Six

        MICK GOWAR

Empty house

You arrive home one night.
You ring the bell (because you're too lazy to get the key out of your pocket!)
No answer.
You ring again.
Still no answer.
Puzzled, you open the door with your key.
The house is empty.
Write the story of the next hour.
In this story, nothing serious happens, except in your imagination. There are no explosions, no murders, no burglars ... nothing more serious than, for example, a telephone ringing or a sound you cannot explain. All the same, you are very relieved when someone turns up, after an hour, shouting, 'I'm home!'.

My Birthday Treat

I was seven years old at the time.
Yet I remember it all so well
In all my sleeping hours still.
I relive that fiery hell.

Mam woke me with excitement.
The Welsh love all bad news.
She thought it would be a treat for me
To give her fair dues.

'Would you like to see a fire
With engines and police too?
Grandad will watch the others.
I came back for you ...'

The middle of the night it was.
Sleep stuck blurred my eyes.
A matter of a minute's walk.
Then feel excitement rise.

Many people stood watching.
Just like Guy Fawkes' Night.
I stood with mouth and eyes wide
At such a terrible sight.

Our sawmills in full flame.
With crackers and Oh's and Ah's.
Eyes like Roman spectators
While moving back their cars.

Then, to my utter terror
A voice shouted, 'Christ, the dogs!'
And I saw my dad disappear
Into the the great, burning, crashing logs.

With the true Welsh sense of drama
The mumbling grew to prayers.
It was all right for the others.
It was my dad, not theirs.

I saw him just for a moment.
Black against the glare.
My heart stopped inside me
For he suddenly wasn't there.

'Dad!' I screamed, and met the eyes.
Heard the tuts of gleeful sympathy.
Such a lovely spectacle it gave
To see terror in such as me.

I felt my mam's arms about me
Then dad he stood right by.
He yelled, 'Why did you bring her, why?
All I could do was cry.

I thought of all the horror,
As I still do each night.
Dad was safe next morning.
But my childhood died of fright.

JOAN M. BATCHELOR

The Vampire

The night is still and sombre,
and in the murky gloom,
arisen from his slumber,
the vampire leaves his tomb.

His eyes are pools of fire,
his skin is icy white,
and blood his one desire
this woebegotten night.

Then through the silent city
he makes his silent way,
prepared to take no pity
upon his hapless prey.

An open window beckons,
he grins a hungry grin,
and pausing not one second
he swiftly climbs within.

And there, beneath her covers,
his victim lies in sleep.
With fangs agleam, he hovers
and with those fangs, bites deep.

The vampire drinks till sated,
he fills his every pore,
and then, his thirst abated,
licks clean the dripping gore.

With powers now replenished,
his thirst no longer burns.
His quest this night is finished,
so to his tomb he turns,

and there awhile in silence
he'll rest beneath the mud
until, with thoughts of violence,
he wakes and utters ... blood!

JACK PRELUTSKY

Questions

If you wanted to find out if someone had understood Jack Prelutsky's poem about a vampire the simplest way would be to ask them a few questions about it.

a   Write down the questions you would want to ask someone about this poem.

b   When you have set them, swap them with another member of your group.

c   Have a go at writing answers to each other's questions.

d   When you have answered them, write some short comments, saying what you thought of the questions you had to answer.

e   Swap back so that you have your own questions again with the answers and the comments. Read it all carefully.

f   As a class, discuss what you've learned from setting your own questions.

At First It Didn't Matter

at first it didn't matter
that rather than talk with me
you preferred to watch the horror films
at night on ITV

at first it didn't matter
but it started getting scary
when your canines started growing
and your hands became all hairy

that I didn't realize earlier
I've only myself to thank
since your family name is Instein
and your father's name is Frank

I should have understood
why on quiet evenings in
whenever I'd try to kiss you
you'd aim below my chin

and the bottles on your doorstep
– you've never really said
why one of them had milk in
but the other two were red

one evening after dinner
I thought music would be nice
so I looked through your records
– they were all by Vincent Price

I asked about your favourite group
you said you weren't selective
you liked all the major groups
– but especially Rhesus Negative

you say your mummy's shy
and I must admit it shows
because of all the bandages
I've only seen her nose

she offered me some coffee
and I'm sorry I caused trouble
but I'd never had it green
and full of steam and bubbles

that was the point I realized
I couldn't take any more
so I fought my way through the vampire bats
and creaked open your huge front door

they say you've got a new boyfriend
they say you fell for his teeth
that he buys clothes in Transylvania
and sends you flowers in wreaths

you go to all the places
we used to hang around
– the difference is with him
you both hang upside down

MIKE STARKEY

Comparisons

Compare this vampire with the one in Jack Prelutsky's poem on the previous pages.

A simple way to start is by listing what each vampire is like and what it does.

Those lists give you some facts about the poems but they don't tell you anything about the way the two poets treat their subject.

What kind of effect do you think the two writers are looking for in their readers?

Which poem do you prefer and why?

Colonel Fazackerley

Colonel Fazackerley Butterworth-Toast
Bought an old castle complete with a ghost,
But someone or other forgot to declare
To Colonel Fazack that the spectre was there.

On the very first evening, while waiting to dine,
The Colonel was taking a fine sherry wine,
When the ghost, with a furious flash and a flare,
Shot out of the chimney and shivered, 'Beware!'

Colonel Fazackerley put down his glass
And said, 'My dear fellow, that's really first class!
I just can't conceive how you do it at all.
I imagine you're going to a Fancy Dress Ball?'

At this, the dread ghost gave a withering cry.
Said the Colonel (his monocle firm in his eye),
'Now just how do you do it I wish I could think.
Do sit down and tell me, and please have a drink.'

The ghost in is phosphorous cloak gave a roar
And floated about between ceiling and floor.
He walked through a wall and returned through a pane
And backed up the chimney and came down again.

Said the Colonel, 'With laughter I'm feeling quite weak!'
(As trickles of merriment ran down his cheek).
'My house-warming party I hope you won't spurn.
You *must* say you'll come and you'll give us a turn!'

At this, the poor spectre – quite out of his wits –
Proceeded to shake himself almost to bits.
He rattled his chains and he clattered his bones
And he filled the whole castle with mumbles and moans.

But Colonel Fazackerley, just as before,
Was simply delighted and called out, 'Encore!'
At which the ghost vanished, his efforts in vain,
And never was seen at the castle again.

'Oh dear, what a pity!' said Colonel Fazack.
'I don't know his name, so I can't call him back.'
And then with a smile that was hard to define,
Colonel Fazackerley went in to dine.

CHARLES CAUSLEY

Thinking it over

a How does Colonel Fazackerley react to the ghost?

b What does the ghost do in response to Colonel Fazackerley's behaviour?

c What sort of cry do you think a 'withering' cry is?

d What do you think that the 'trickles of merriment' are?

e Find another word, in the poem, for a ghost.

f Why do you think the Colonel smiled as he went into dinner?

The Way Through the Woods

They shut the road through the woods
Seventy years ago.
Weather and rain have undone it again,
And now you would never know
There was once a road through the woods
Before they planted the trees.
It is underneath the coppice and heath,
And the thin anemones.
Only the keeper sees
That, where the ring-dove broods,
And the badgers roll at ease,
There was once a road through the woods.

Yet, if you enter the woods
Of a summer evening late,
When the night-air cools on the trout-ringed pools
Where the otter whistles his mate
(They fear not men in the woods,
Because they see so few),
You will hear the beat of a horse's feet,
And the swish of a skirt in the dew,
Steadily cantering through
The misty solitudes,
As though they perfectly knew
The old lost road through the woods . . .
But there is no road through the woods!

RUDYARD KIPLING

The Fog

Slowly the fog,
Hunch-shouldered with a grey face,
Arms wide, advances,
Finger-tips touching the way
Past the dark houses
And dark gardens of roses.
Up the short street from the harbour,
Slowly the fog,
Seeking, seeking;
Arms wide, shoulders hunched,
Searching, searching,
Out through the streets to the fields,
Slowly the fog –
A blind man hunting the moon.

F.R. McCREARY

Things are people

Sometimes a writer speaks as if something were actually someone. In F.R. McCreary's poem the fog has become like a human being. What does the poem tell us about this imagined person?

This is your chance to experiment with the idea that things have human qualities. (This kind of writing is not easy so do not be surprised if you are not immediately successful.)

You may have plenty of ideas of your own but if not here are a few things that you might like to imagine as being a person.

TV   Car   Tennis racket

The cold   Bicycle   Coat

Computer   Refrigerator

House   Money

I must be the only person in the world to have fifty owners a day. I've been in so many wallets and purses I'm sick to death of it. Honestly, I think I'm becoming allergic to leather.

Where am I now? In a till in a shop called Tesco. I hate it. The customers shout, the till makes to much noise and all that stacking of tins drives me mad. No wonder I've got a headache . . . . .

Rachelle

Workings of the Wind

Wind doesn't always topple trees
and shake houses to pieces.

Wind plays
all over woods, with weighty ghosts
in swings in thousands,
swinging from every branch.

Wind doesn't always rattle windows
and push, push at walls.

Wind whistles
down cul-de-sacs and worries
dry leaves and old newspapers to leap
and curl like kite tails.

Wind doesn't always dry out
sweaty shirts and blouses.

Wind scatters
pollen dust of flowers, washes
people's and animals' faces
and combs out birds' feathers.

Wind doesn't always whip up waves
into white horses.

Wind shakes up
tree-shadows to dance on rivers,
to jig about on grass, and hanging
lantern light to play signalman.

Wind doesn't always run wild
kicking tinny dustbin lids.

Wind makes
leafy limbs bow to red roses
and bob up and down outside windows
and makes desk papers fly up indoors.

JAMES BERRY

Finding the right words

A large part of being able to write successfully lies in choosing the right words. That is what James Berry has done with great accuracy in his poem about the wind.

Because the wind never remains still, some of the most important words in a description of it are the *verbs* (the words that say what is done.) See if you can find those words in the poem.

Now you may well think that you could never write even one line about the wind as effectively as James Berry. However if you could find the right words, you might well be surprised at your own powers of description.

To help you write about the wind, here are a selection of verbs that might give you ideas for your description.

	splits	bursts	
slams	taps	frightens	
opens	pierces	punches	tunnels
penetrates	crashes	flies	flitters
dances	darts	flaps	leaps
springs	frolics	bounds	careers
demolishes	loosens	writhes	squirms
rushes	quivers	whisks	
	haunts	startles	

Write a series of sentences about what the wind does.

Keep each sentence separate as James Berry does.

When you have finished your first version, read it over and decide the order you want the sentences in your final version.

Rain

The lights are all on, though it's just past midday,
There are no more indoor games we can play,
No one can think of anything to say,
It rained all yesterday, it's raining today,
It's grey outside, inside me it's grey.

I stare out of the window, fist under my chin,
The gutter leaks drips on the lid of the dustbin,
When they say 'cheer up', I manage a grin,
I draw a fish on the glass with a sail-sized fin,
It's sodden outside, and its damp within.

Matches, bubbles and papers pour into the drains,
Clouds smother the sad laments from the trains,
Grandad says it brings on his rheumatic pains,
The moisture's got right inside of my brains,
It's raining outside, inside me it rains.

BRIAN LEE

Thinking it over

a   Why are the lights on in the writer's house?

b   What has the writer been doing?

c   What effect does the weather have on Grandad?

d   What effect does the weather have on the writer?

A couple of dull wet days and people begin saying that they have got 'nothing to do'.

Usually this means that they have done all the things they like doing until they're bored silly with them. That only leaves things which cannot be done when it's raining or things which they don't want to do.

See if you can capture the boredom of wet weather in your own piece of writing called 'Nothing to do'. You might like to use the title as a *refrain* (a repeated phrase) which comes up regularly in your piece.

If you're not sure how to start think about it in three ways:
(i)   all the things you do on a wet day.
(ii)   all the things you'd prefer to be doing.
(iii)   all the things you don't like doing but might get roped into because it's a wet day.

Sky in the Pie!

Waiter, there's a sky in my pie
Remove it at once if you please
You can keep your incredible sunsets
I ordered mincemeat and cheese

I can't stand nightingales singing
Or clouds all burnished with gold
The whispering breeze is disturbing the peas
And making my chips go all cold

I don't care if the chef is an artist
Whose canvases hang in the Tate
I want two veg. and puff pastry
Not the Universe heaped on my plate

OK I'll try just a spoonful
I suppose I've got nothing to lose
Mm ... the colours quite tickle the palette
With a blend of delicate hues

The sun has a custardy flavour
And the clouds are as light as air
And the wind a chewier texture
(With a hint of cinnamon there?)

This sky is simply delicious
Why haven't I tried it before?
I can chew my way through Eternity
And still have room left for more

Having acquired a taste for the Cosmos
I'll polish this sunset off soon
I can't wait to tuck into the night sky
Waiter! Please bring me the Moon!

ROGER McGOUGH

The Stunning Great Meat Pie

You've heard of the wondrous crocodile
  And the thundering great sea snake,
No doubt it's often made you smile,
  And caused your sides to ache;
Now I've got one that'll make you laugh
  For a month to come, or nigh –
So listen while I tell you about
  A stunning great meat pie.

Now hungry folk can eat a horse –
  So I hope you'll swallow this tale,
Of the thirty-thousand-portion pie
  Cooked up in Denby Dale!

You may guess it was a tidy size,
  It took a week to make it;
A day to carry it to the shop,
  And just a week to bake it.
Oh! had you seen it, I'll be bound,
  Your wonder you'd scarce govern;
They were forced to break the front wall down
  To get it to the oven.

It took full thirty sacks of flour,
  It's a fact that now I utter,
Three hundred pails of water too,
  And a hundred tubs of butter.
The crust was nearly seven feet thick,
  You couldn't easily bruise it;
And the rolling pin was such a size
  That it took twelve men to use it!

There were twenty-five spare-ribs of pork,
  I'm sure I'm not mistaken;
With two-and-thirty hams from York,
  And twenty sides of bacon.
The pie was made by fifty cooks –
  And all of them first-raters!
And then they filled up all the nooks
  With a ton of kidney taters!

When word was given a general rush
  Took place to hack and hew it;
They clambered up outside the crust
  To get their knives into it.
When all at once the crust gave way,
  It's true, I'll take my davy!
And ninety-five poor souls, they say,
  Were drowned in the gravy!

ANON

Titling

Like many poems, this one is broken into seperate verses.

See if you can give each verse of the poem a title which helps to explain what that verse is about.

If you manage to do that successfully, you'll have a good idea of the way the writer has organized the poem.

Finally, find an alternative title for this story that could be used as a newspaper headline.

Poisoning People is Wrong

You've done it again haven't you?
You've eaten the cherries
And given the rest of your cake to the rabbit.

I SAY NOTHING.

And who gave the crust of the pork pie
To the dog?
Who?
I'll bet it was you.
He's been sick twice this morning you know.

ALL THE MORE REASON
FOR ME NOT TO EAT IT.

I keep finding crusts all over the house.
You're supposed to eat the whole of the bread
Not shove the bits you don't like in your pocket
And stick them in the bookcase later on.
I'd sniffed my way around
Fourteen Dickens' novels
Before I found your rotten crusts.
They'd gone green.
Are you listening?
Green, they'd gone.

SO SHE'S DESTROYED MY PENICILLIN FACTORY.
SHE HATES SCIENTISTS.

As for that cabbage:
If you'd said you didn't want it
I wouldn't have given you so much.
You're disgusting you are.

WELL SOMETHING WAS NEEDED
TO FILL THAT GAP AT THE
BACK OF THE SOFA.

Baked potatoes
Are meant to be eaten
Not be poked about
And don't leave the skin this time:
That's the bit with all the vitamins.

THAT'S ALSO THE BIT WITH
ALL THE MUD IF SHE'S LEFT
MY FATHER TO SCRUB THEM.

Yes, we are having rice pudding for afters
And, yes, you do have to eat it.
In my day
You were grateful if you got rice pudding.
In my day
Things were different.

IN HER DAY IT WAS ILLEGAL TO POISON
CHILDREN.

Are you muttering something?

ME? NOT ME?

                        DAVID KITCHEN

The 'Veggy' Lion

I'm a vegetarian Lion,
I've given up all meat,
I've given up all roaring
All I do is go tweet-tweet.

I never ever sink my claws
Into some animal's skin,
It only lets the blood run out
And lets the germs rush in.

I used to be ferocious,
I even tried to kill!
But the sight of all that blood
Made me feel quite ill.

I once attacked an Elephant
I sprang straight at his head.
I woke up three days later
In a Jungle hospital bed.

Now I just eat carrots,
They're easier to kill,
'Cos when I pounce upon them,
They all remain quite still!

SPIKE MILLIGAN

The Apple Raid

Darkness came early, though not yet cold;
Stars were strung on the telegraph wires;
Street lamps spilled pools of liquid gold;
The breeze was spiced with garden fires.

That smell of burnt leaves, the early dark,
Can still excite me but not as it did
So long ago when we met in the park –
Myself, John Peters and David Kidd.

We moved out of town to the district where
The lucky and wealthy had their homes
With garages, gardens, and apples to spare
Ripely clustered in the trees' green domes.

We chose the place we meant to plunder
And climbed the wall and dropped down to
The secret dark. Apples crunched under
Our feet as we moved through the grass and dew.

The clusters on the lower boughs of the tree
Were easy to reach. We stored the fruit
In pockets and jerseys until all three
Boys were heavy with their tasty loot.

Safe on the other side of the wall
We moved back to town and munched as we went.
I wonder if David remembers at all
That little adventure, the apples' fresh scent.

Strange to think that he's fifty years old,
That tough little boy with scabs on his knees;
Stranger to think that John Peters lies cold
In an orchard in France beneath apple trees.

VERNON SCANNELL

Thinking it over

a About what time of the day is the poet writing?

b Where did the boys go to steal apples?

c Why are the trees described as having 'green domes'?

d In verse four, what does the word 'plunder' mean?

e What has happened to the poet's friends?

Describe the stealing of the apples in your own words, imagining that you were one of the group.

Portrait of a House

The house that we live in was built in a place
That was once a mere cube of unoccupied space;
And the birds that flew through it and passed on their way
Would collide with a wall or a window to-day.

The rooms in the house are of medium size,
The sort that an ant would regard with surprise;
While a whale could express no opinion at all,
For his bulk would prevent him from passing the hall.

The stairs are arranged with such exquisite skill
That a person can climb or descend them at will;
And the absence of rain from the attics is proof
That the architect thought of supplying a roof.

Of the doors and the windows our only complaint
Is the fact that you can't see the wood for the paint:
A trouble with which we've decided to deal
By allowing the paint to continue to peel.

The chairs and the tables are perfectly tame,
And to speak of them harshly is rather a shame;
But nevertheless I am bound to remark
On their savage resistance when bumped in the dark.

In the kitchen, in spite of its tropical clime,
Two cats and a cook spend the whole of their time.
The cats have been known to meander about,
But the cook is a fixture and never goes out.

It is said that mysterious sounds may be heard
In the house when it's empty; but this is absurd.
If you've gone there to listen, it's clear to a dunce
That the house will have ceased to be empty at once.

We've a spare-room prepared for the casual guest,
But it really is not what the name would suggest;
For although it's a room, it is never to spare,
As someone or other is constantly there.

I have made it quite clear that our chosen abode
Is different from all of the rest in the road –
What a beautiful house for play, dinner and slumber!
And yet to the postman it's only a number.

E.V. RIEU

Description

a   It's no easy task, describing your home.
Could you take a stranger in a tour in words of where you live?
Perhaps a good place to start is the setting.
What is the road like in which you live?
Write a sentence or two. No more.
Pause. Read it over. Can it be improved?

b   **Now, what does the building look like from the outside?**
Think about the building's colour, the condition, the doors, the windows, the garden if there
is one, the age.
Write it down.
Pause. Read it over. Can it be improved?

c   Let's walk up the path.
Open the door.
What do you see?
One sentence only.
Check it over.

d   Step inside.
Now where will you take your visitor?
Will you show him the posh bits or the tatty bits?
Start in one room. Point out two or three things.
Not the obvious ones like the new telly on the coffee table but the dead spider behind the
wedding photograph or the mark on the carpet left by the chemistry experiment you did when
everyone was out.
Write as much as you like.
Pause. Read it over. Are any changes needed?

e   Where would you go next in the house?
The room where your cousin stayed when she came from Nigeria?
The cupboard where dad's home-made beer exploded?
Keep thinking and writing about a variety of things until you feel you've
captured a little of the flavour of your home.
Don't forget that homes are made up of people and memories not just floors and walls.

f   When you think you've finished, read it all over.
Does it flow?
Perhaps it needs one or two sentences to link it together.
Perhaps some parts need cutting down or cutting out altogether.
Make those decisions *before* you start your final version.

Socks

My local Gents' Outfitter stocks
The latest line in snazzy socks:
Black socks, white socks,
Morning, noon and night socks,
Grey socks, green socks,
Small, large and in between socks,
Blue socks, brown socks,
Always-falling-down socks,
Orange socks, red socks,
Baby socks and bed socks;
Purple socks, pink socks,
What-would-people-think socks,
Holey socks and frayed socks,
British Empire-made socks,
Long socks, short socks,
Any-sort-of-sport socks,
Thick socks, thin socks,
And 'these-have-just-come-in' socks.

Socks with stripes and socks with spots,
Socks with stars and polka dots,
Socks for ankles, socks for knees,
Socks with twelve-month guarantees,
Socks for aunties, socks for uncles,
Socks to cure you of carbuncles,
Socks for nephews, socks for nieces,
Socks that won't show up their creases,
Socks whose colour glows fluorescent,
Socks for child or adolescent,
Socks for ladies, socks for gents,
Socks for only fifty pence.

Socks for winter, socks for autumn,
Socks with garters to support 'em.
Socks for work and socks for leisure,
Socks hand-knitted, made-to-measure,
Socks of wool and polyester,
Socks from Lincoln, Leeds and Leicester,
Socks of cotton and elastic,
Socks of paper, socks of plastic,
Socks of silk-embroidered satin,
Socks with mottoes done in Latin,
Socks for soldiers in the army,
Socks to crochet or macramé,
Socks for destinations distant,
Shrink-proof, stretch-proof, heat-resistant.

Baggy socks, brief socks,
Union Jack motif socks,
Chequered socks, tartan socks.
School or kindergarten socks,
Sensible socks, silly socks,
Frivolous and frilly socks,
Impractical socks, impossible socks,
Drip-dry machine-only-washable socks,
Bulgarian socks, Brazilian socks,
There seem to be over a million socks!

With all these socks, there's just one catch –
It's hard to find a pair that match.

COLIN WEST

Noise

I like noise.
The whoop of a boy, the thud of a hoof,
The rattle of rain on a galvanized roof,
The hubbub of traffic, the roar of a train,
The throb of machinery numbing the brain,
The rush of the wind, a door on the slam,
The switching of wires in an overhead tram,
The boom of the thunder, the crash of the waves,
The din of a river that races and raves,
The crack of a rifle, the clank of a pail,
The strident tattoo of a swift-slapping sail –
Arises a gamut of soul-stirring joys.
I like noise.

JESSIE POPE

Noise Words

How many words can you think of that suggest noise?

Jot down as many as you can including those you can find in the poem.

Look at the different sounds they suggest.

What words of your own can you make up that suggest a sound?

See if you can write your own short poem purely out of sound words.

Don't worry too much about the meaning on this occasion, just concentrate on the sound and the way it flows.

The Paint Box

'Cobalt and umber and ultramarine,
Ivory black and emerald green –
What shall I paint to give pleasure to you?'
'Paint for me somebody utterly new.'

'I have painted you tigers in crimson and white,'
'The colours were good and you painted aright.'
'I have painted the cook and a camel in blue
And a panther in purple.' 'You painted them true.

Now mix me a colour that nobody knows,
And paint me a country where nobody goes,
And put in it people a little like you,
Watching a unicorn drinking the dew.'

E.V. RIEU

Swap? Sell? Small Ads Sell Fast

1950 Dad. Good runner; needs one or
Two repairs; a few grey hairs but
Nothing a respray couldn't fix
Would like a 1966 five-speed turbo
In exchange: something in the sporty
Twin-carb range.

LUXURIOUS Leather 3-piece suite, ex "World of Leather", dark brown, excellent condition £695. — Ring 142 4074 (after 5.30 p.m.)
G-2-6
LUXURY HARDWOOD Flooring, stock clearance from £5.50 yd. — Tel. 195-8633.
L-2-9

LOUNGE three piece suite, unused, dralon velvet, high back, £199, can deliver. — 955 3508.
L-2-7
PIANO WORLD Sale. One of London's largest selections of new and reconditioned pianos. Uprights/grands. Hire now, buy later. Open 7 days. — 199 Chalk Farm Road. London NW1. — 01-285 1555
0-2-11

COLOUR T.V., old style but working order, hence £22. — Tel. 173 2829.
COOKER, gas, modern, white, 4 rings, large oven, grill at the top, superb condition, could deliver, £24. — Phone after 7 p.m. any day 01-228 4292. Victoria.

1920s Granny. Not many like this
In such clean and rust-free state.
You must stop by to view! All chrome
As new, original fascia retained
Upholstery unstained. Passed MOT
Last week: will only swap for some-
Thing quite unique.

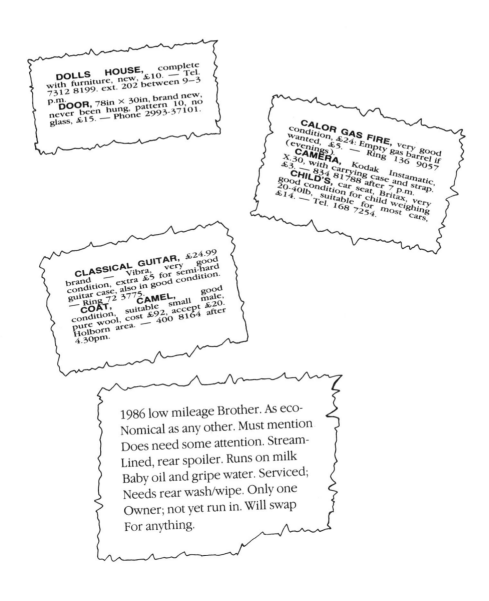

DOLLS HOUSE, complete with furniture, new, £10. — Tel. 7312 8199. ext. 202 between 9–3 p.m.

DOOR, 78in × 30in, brand new, never been hung, pattern 10, no glass, £15. — Phone 2993-37101.

CALOR GAS FIRE, very good condition, £24: Empty gas barrel if wanted, £5. — Ring 136 9057 (evenings).

CAMERA, Kodak Instamatic, X.30, with carrying case and strap. £3. — 834 81788 after 7 p.m.

CHILD'S, car seat, Britax, very good condition for child weighing 20-40lb, suitable for most cars, £14. — Tel. 168 7254.

CLASSICAL GUITAR, £24.99 brand — Vibra, very good condition, extra £5 for semi-hard guitar case, also in good condition. — Ring 72 3775.

COAT, CAMEL, good condition, suitable small male, pure wool, cost £92, accept £20. Holborn area. — 400 8164 after 4.30pm.

1986 low mileage Brother. As eco-
Nomical as any other. Must mention
Does need some attention. Stream-
Lined, rear spoiler. Runs on milk
Baby oil and gripe water. Serviced;
Needs rear wash/wipe. Only one
Owner; not yet run in. Will swap
For anything.

TREVOR MILLUM

For Sale

Suppose schools were able to buy and sell their pupils.

Who would you put up for sale and how would you advertise them?

Specimen

And this is our rarest specimen of all:
The last living human
Oh, you can see their bones in museums,
I know that,
But you will be one of the last of our community
To see one alive.

Yes, there were millions of them once.
I've heard my grandfather speak of
Hunting them for sport,
A fine sport, too,
And fair;
Never more than six wolves to the hunt
So the human had a chance.

Cruel?
I don't think so.
They were hunters themselves, you know.
Our history says that
As the size of their weapons increased
The size of their brains got smaller.

No, personally, I don't believe that.
There's another theory that one of their weapons
Caused horrible changes,
Killed many of them and left their children
And their children's children different,
Helpless.
The history books find that too fanciful
But I wouldn't be too sure.

Oh, it has to be behind those bars
For its safety
And it certainly wouldn't survive
In the wild, anymore.
It's kindness really and,
Being a dumb human
It doesn't really understand its situation.

The eyes?
Oh, the eyes often water like that
It's part of the cleansing mechanism
For its vision.
Very effective, I believe,
But of no further significance.
Sad?
Well, yes I suppose it is
But that's progress isn'tit?

DAVID KITCHEN

Thinking it over

a Where does this poem take place?

b What do you imagine happened to the human race?

c Who or what do you think may have now taken over the world?

d Why does the speaker think that there is nothing particularly cruel about the way the last human is treated?

Imagine you are the last human.
What is life like behind those bars?
What sort of daily routine is there?
How are you treated?
How are you fed?
How are you clothed?
What are the reactions of those who see you?
How were you capured?
What was life like in the wild?
What do you remember of the history of your race?

(*Don't* answer all these questions a sentence at a time. They are just to help you to start thinking about what it is like to be the last human being.)

The Computer's First Christmas Card

jollymerry
hollyberry
jollyberry
merryholly
happyjolly
jollyjelly
jellybelly
bellymerry
hollyheppy
jollyMolly
marryJerry
merryHarry
hoppyBarry
heppyJarry
boppyheppy
berryjorry
jorryjolly
moppyjelly
Mollymerry
Jerryjolly
bellyboppy
jorryhoppy
hollymoppy
Barrymerry
Jarryhappy
happyboppy
boppyjolly
jollymerry
merrymerry
merrymerry
merryChris
ammerryasa
Chrismerry
asMERRYCHR
YSANTHEMUM

EDWIN
MORGAN

Computer's Greetings

What would be the result if a computer got its micro chips into other cards?
What might happen to one or more of these greetings?

> Happy birthday
> Congratulations
> Best wishes
> Many happy returns
> Be my Valentine
> Get well soon

Southbound on the Freeway

A tourist came in from Orbitville,
parked in the air, and said:

The creatures of this star
are made of metal and glass.

Through the transparent parts
you can see their guts.

Their feet are round and roll
on diagrams or long

measuring tapes, dark
with white lines.

They have four eyes.
The two in back are red.

Sometimes you can see a five-eyed
one, with a red eye turning

on the top of his head.
He must be special –

and others respect him
and go slow

when he passes, winding
among them from behind.

They all hiss as they glide,
like inches, down the marked

tapes. Those soft shapes,
shadowy inside

the hard bodies – are they
their guts or their brains?

MAY SWENSON

Entertaining an Orbitvillian

Imagine the alien from Orbitville discovers that he can understand human speech. Looking around for someone who can explain things to him, he focuses in on you because you're speaking louder and longer than anyone else in the neighbourhood.

Being a friendly sort of person, you take your alien guest home. What happens?

Remember that this newcomer from Orbitville will be confused by a hundred and one aspects of our life and wants to know everything.

Here are just a few possibilities of areas of confusion:

hair
TV
politicians
shops
religion
washing machines
babies
fires
school
beds
holidays
war

I Had Rather Be A Woman

I had rather be a woman
Than an earwig
But there's not much in it sometimes.
We both crawl out of bed
But there the likeness ends.
Earwigs don't have to
Feed their children,
Feed the cat,
Feed the rabbits,
Feed the dishwasher.
They don't need
Clean sheets,
Clean clothes,
Clean carpets.
A clean bill of health.
They just rummage about
In chrysanthemums.
No one expects them
To have their
Teetotal, vegetarian
Mothers-in-law
To stay for Christmas,
Or to feel a secret thrill
At the thought of extending the kitchen.
Earwigs can snap their pincers at life
And scurry about being quite irresponsible.
They enjoy an undeserved reputation
Which frightens the boldest child.
Next time I feel hysterical
I'll bite a hole in a dahlia.

DAPHNE SCHILLER

Who we are and what we are is, in many ways, decided by our birth.

In spite of this, we spend enormous amounts of time imagining what it would be like to be someone else or something else.

What would you prefer to be and why?

Write a piece that starts 'I'd rather be . . . .'

Claims

My father had a motor car:
It was his pride and joy.
He would have taught me how to drive
If I had been a boy.

But girls grow into women
And women are to blame,
According to my father,
For each insurance claim.

We're just not built for things like cars.
Dad says we mustn't moan:
Men are built for speed and strength,
Women for the home.

My mother used to drive a bit
Until the accident:
Parking in the multi-storey,
A wing mirror got bent.

It wasn't really Mum's fault,
There simply wasn't space.
You'd think to hear my father rant
She'd damned the human race.

My mother didn't argue,
She says she saves her breath,
Dad homes in for a blazing row
Like vultures swoop on death.

'Women drivers,' said my dad
'No one need discuss:
Women should accept their lot
And meekly take the bus.'

Which makes it such a pity,
Such wretched awful luck,
That Dad has driven his new car
Half way up a truck.

What makes it worse in Dad's eyes
(And the police's book)
Is that the truck was neatly parked
And father didn't look.

His seat belt meant that he was safe,
Though the car's beyond repair;
What hurt him was the firemen laughed
As they cut him free from there.

He sometimes takes the subject up,
Explains the crash away.
My Mum and I say nothing,
Much to Dad's dismay.

But part of what Dad taught me,
I must admit, remains:
Men are built with speed and strength
But hardly any brains.

DAVID KITCHEN

The Changeling

Mary's mother is tall and fair,
Her father is freckled with ginger hair,
And they live in a house all polished and neat
In the very centre of Riverside Street.

But Mary is dark and thin and wild,
And she doesn't laugh like a human child,
And she doesn't cry like you and me
With tears as salt as the brooding sea.

For when Mary giggles the rattling sound
Is worse than the traffic for miles around;
And the sobs that heave Mary's shoulders high,
Leave her throat parched and her wide eyes dry.

In the classroom Mary works on her own,
And she plays in the playground quite alone.
In church she will not pray or sing,
For she never will join in anything.

It can only be that ten years ago,
In hurtling sleet and blinding snow,
Some dreaming wizards or spiteful elves
Went cradle-swapping to please themselves.

Took the real Mary to join their race
And left their fledgling, in her place,
To grow both beautiful and sly
With power to destroy in her evil eye.

And the only thing both Marys share
Is that they are homesick everywhere.
So sumptuously by the fairies fed,
The one is hungry for human bread.

The other however the heat's turned higher
Is cold for the lack of fairy fire.
And the parents cannot know what is meant
By their daughter's waspish discontent.

Her sulks and tempers are never done,
She's a stock of harsh words for everyone;
While they, dismayed by their puzzling fate,
Go to bed early and get up late.

So now the mother is bent and grey,
And the father sits in his chair all day,
And Riverside Street cannot abide
The slum that their house has become inside.

SHIRLEY TOULSON

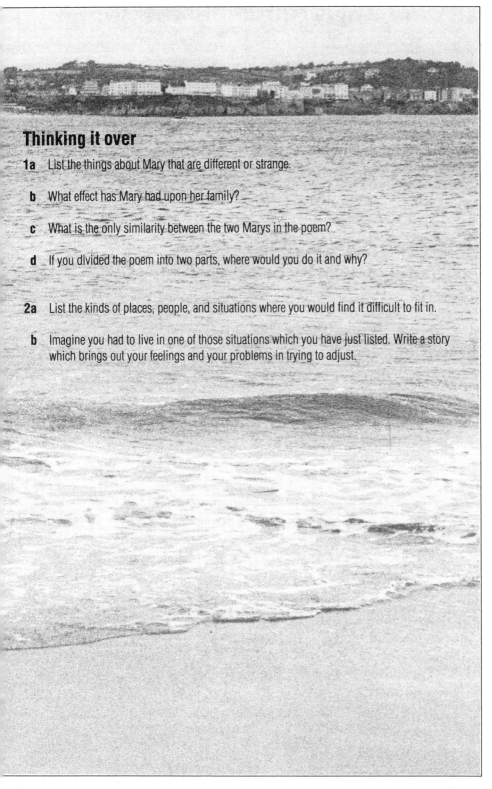

Thinking it over

1a List the things about Mary that are different or strange.

b What effect has Mary had upon her family?

c What is the only similarity between the two Marys in the poem?

d If you divided the poem into two parts, where would you do it and why?

2a List the kinds of places, people, and situations where you would find it difficult to fit in.

b Imagine you had to live in one of those situations which you have just listed. Write a story which brings out your feelings and your problems in trying to adjust.

Angel Hill

A sailor came walking down Angel Hill,
He knocked on my door with a right good will,
With a right good will he knocked on my door.
He said, 'My friend, we have met before.'
     No, never, said I.

He searched my eye with a sea-blue stare
And he laughed aloud on the Cornish air,
On the Cornish air he laughed aloud
And he said, 'My friend, you have grown too proud.'
     No, never, said I.

'In war we swallowed the bitter bread
And drank of the brine,' the sailor said.
'We took of the bread and we tasted the brine
As I bound your wounds and you bound mine.'
     No, never, said I.

'By day and night on the diving sea
We whistled to sun and moon,' said he.
'Together we whistled to moon and sun
And vowed our stars should be as one.'
     No, never, said I.

'And now,' he said, 'that the war is past
I come to your hearth and home at last.
I come to your home and hearth to share
Whatever fortune waits me there.'
     No, never, said I.

'I have no wife nor son,' he said,
'Nor pillow on which to lay my head,
No pillow have I, nor wife nor son,
Till you shall give to me my own.'
     No, never, said I.

His eye it flashed like a lightning-dart
And still as stone then stood my heart.
My heart as a granite stone was still
And he said, 'My friend, but I think you will.'
     No, never, said I.

The sailor smiled and turned in his track
And shifted the bundle on his back
And I heard him sing as he strolled away,
'You'll send and you'll fetch me one fine day.'
     No, never, said I.

CHARLES CAUSLEY

Thinking it over

a What mood is the sailor in when he knocks on the writer's door?

b What experiences have they shared, according to the sailor?

c Why does the sailor come to visit the writer?

d What do we learn about the sailor's family?

e What response does the sailor receive to his visit?

f Has the writer really never met the sailor before? What do you think?

g The sailor walks away and the writer turns back into his home and his family. His wife says: 'Who was that . . .'
Imagine the conversation between the writer and his family.

Snow Towards Evening

Suddenly the sky turned grey,
The day,
Which had been bitter and chill,
Grew soft and still.
Quietly
From some invisible blossoming tree
Millions of petals cool and white
Drifted and blew,
Lifted and flew,
Fell with the falling night.

MELVILLE CANE

Snow Haiku

Probably this will not be the first time you have been asked to describe snow. Although the first part of the work may be familiar to you, the end result will be rather different.

STEP ONE
First of all, we want to get as much down on paper about snow as we can, relatively quickly. Think about the look and the feel of snow. What are the effects of it and what can be done with it?

STEP TWO
You should now have an adequate standard description of snow.
Most average descriptions say very little about what snow is *like*.
    What does the snow look like?
    What are the roads like when covered by snow?
    What is it like to watch the very first flakes fall?
    What is it like to be out walking in a snowstorm?
See what you can add to your description.

STEP THREE
By now you should have a piece of writing that needs to be organized again.
Instead of writing it all out and just changing the order, we're going to change the description into the form of a *haiku*, a tiny Japanese poem.
A haiku has five syllables in the first line, seven in the second and five in the third. (If you're not sure what a syllable is, just ask.)

Here's one example of a haiku.

> The snow falls gently,
> Powder white, drifting downward
> Softly, silently

Can you take the very best out of your description and fit it into three short lines?
See what you can manage.

(There's no rule that says you must write only one haiku; write as many as you wish and see which you prefer.)

Boy at the Window

Seeing the snowman standing all alone
In the dusk and cold is more than he can bear.
The small boy weeps to hear the wind prepare
A night of gnashings and enormous moan.
His tearful sight can hardly reach to where
The pale-faced figure with bitumen eyes
Returns him such a god-forsaken stare
As outcast Adam gave Paradise.

The man of snow is, nonetheless, content,
Having no wish to go inside and die.
Still, he is moved to see the youngster cry.
Though frozen water is his element,
He melts enough to drop from one soft eye
A trickle of the purest rain, a tear
For the child at the bright pane surrounded by
Such warmth, such light, such love, and so much fear.

RICHARD WILBUR

The Longest Journey in the World

'Last one into bed
has to switch out the light.'
It's just the same every night.
There's a race.
I'm ripping off my trousers and shirt,
he's kicking off his shoes and socks.

'My sleeve's stuck.'
'This button's too big for its button-hole.'
'Have you hidden my pyjamas?'
'Keep your hands off mine.'

If you win
you get where it's safe
before the darkness comes –
but if you lose
if you're last
you know what you've got coming up is
the journey from the light switch to your bed.
It's the Longest Journey in the World.

'You're last tonight,' my brother says.
And he's right.

There is nowhere so dark
as that room in the moment
after I've switched out the light.

There is nowhere so full of dangerous things,
things that love dark places,
things that breathe only when you breathe
and hold their breath when I hold mine.

So I have to say:
'I'm not scared.'
That face, grinning in the pattern on the wall,
isn't a face –
'I'm not scared.'
That prickle on the back of my neck
is only the label on my pyjama jacket –
'I'm not scared.'
That moaning-moaning is nothing
but water in a pipe –
'I'm not scared.'

Everything's going to be just fine
as soon as I get into that bed of mine.
Such a terrible shame
it's always the same
it takes so long
it takes so long
it takes so long
to get there.

From the light switch
to my bed
it's the Longest Journey in the World.

MICHAEL ROSEN

Alone in the Dark

She has taken out the candle,
She has left me in the dark;
From the window not a glimmer,
From the fireplace not a spark.

I am frightened as I'm lying
All alone here in my bed,
And I've wrapped the clothes as closely
As I can around my head.

But what is it makes me tremble?
And why should I fear the gloom?
I am certain there is nothing
In the corners of the room.

ANON

Just in case . . .

Of course, there is nothing to fear in the darkness, is there?

The sound you can hear is just a floorboard creaking.

The horrible gurgling noise comes from next door's water system.

The grotesque low moaning sound is the one grandpa always makes when he falls asleep lying on his back.

And you don't really want to go to the toilet. You can wait until the morning. If you close your eyes you'll forget that you want to go . . . or will you?

Write a piece which starts with you under the covers . . . but needing to get out of bed . . . but not wanting to in case, well, just in case . . .

Why English is So Hard

We'll begin with a box, and the plural is boxes;
But the plural of ox should be oxen, not oxes.
Then one fowl is goose, but two are called geese;
Yet the plural of moose should never be meese.
You may find a lone mouse or a whole lot of mice,
By the plural of house is houses, not hice.
If the plural of man is always called men,
Why shouldn't the plural of pan be called pen?
The cow in the plural may be cows or kine,
But the plural of vow is vows, not vine.
And I speak of a foot, and you show me your feet,
But I give you a boot – would a pair be called beet?
If one is a tooth and a whole set are teeth,
Why shouldn't the plural of booth be called beeth?
If the singular is this, and the plural is these,
Should the plural of kiss be nicknamed kese?
Then one may be that, and three may be those,
Yet the plural of hat would never be hose.
We speak of a brother, and also of brethren,
But though we say mother, we never say methren.
The masculine pronouns are he, his, and him,
But imagine the feminine she, shis, and shim!
So our English, I think you will all agree,
Is the trickiest language you ever did see.

ANON

If...

If ships sailed on the motorway
   And potato crisps were blue,
If football boots were made of silk
   And a lamp-post wore a shoe;
If motorbikes ran upwards
   And milk floats really floated,
If beds were full of boulders
   And peas were sugar coated;
If flies wore army jackets
   And eggs laid little chickens,
If spacemen had a panther each
   And insects studied Dickens;
If babies' prams were motorised
   And you listened to your conscience,
If life was always back to front
   You wouldn't read this nonscience!

JOHN RICE

WHERE TO FIND THE MATERIAL

Poem in **advertisement** form 84–85.

Poems about **animals** 9–19, 76, 86–87.

Written work in the form of **conversation** 22–23, 31, 98–99.

Poems about **death** 14–19

Opportunities to prepare **descriptive** writing 6, 9–12, 48–49, 68–70, 78–79.

Material that emphasises **drafting** ix–x, 2–4, 78–79.

Poems about **family** 5, 22–23, 53–57, 60–61, 74–76, 78–79, 84–85, 92–99, 104–105.

Opportunities to write **fantasy** 30, 36–38, 45, 66–67, 84–93, 104–106.

Poems about **fear** 52–59, 104–106.

Poems about **food** 1, 71–77.

Poems about the **future** 86–91.

Opportunity to write **Haiku** 100–102.

Work which involves a strong element of **humour**, (particularly suitable for the last lesson of a wet windy Thursday) 26, 30, 40–43, 45, 84–85.

Poems about **identity** 2–8.

Poems about **memories** 16–19, 31, 53, 56–57, 77, 98–99.

Poems about **mystery** 58–64, 98–99

Narrative poetry 18–19, 32–33, 52, 56–57, 72–73, 77, 96–99.

Poems concerning **nature** 64–70, 100–103.

Paired poems. With assignments that specifically link the poems 9–12, 58–61, 100–102, 104–106.
Without linking assignments 13–14, 16–19, 39–41, 45–46, 52–53.

Poems about **parents** 20–21, 56–57, 74–75.

Poems about **people** 31–35, 53.

Opportunities to write from **personal** experience 2–4, 22–23, 27–29, 54, 96–97, 104–106.

Opportunity to attempt **personnification** 66–67.

Opportunities to write **poetry** 3–5, 42–43, 50–51, 68, 70, 82, 88–89 100–102.

Poems with a **puzzle** element 46–51, 90–91.

Opportunities to solve linguistic **puzzles** 46–51.

INDEX OF AUTHORS

ACKNOWLEDGEMENTS

The editor and publishers wish to thank the following for permission to reproduce copyright material. It has not been possible to contact all copyright holders, and the publishers would be glad to hear from any unacknowledged sources.

Marian Reiner and the author for 'How to Eat a Poem' from *Jamboree: Rhymes for All Times* by Eve Merriam © 1962, 1964, 1973, 1984; Fontana Young Lions, an imprint of the Collins Group, for 'Me' from *Rabbiting On* by Kit Wright © Kit Wright 1978; William Collins Sons & Co Ltd for 'Coming Home' from *Swings and Roundabouts* by Mick Gowar © Mick Gowar 1981; Penguin Books Ltd for 'A Boy's Head' by Miroslav Holub from *Penguin Modern European Poets*, 1967 © Miroslav Holub 1967, translation © Penguin Books 1967; Deborah Rogers Ltd and Gareth Owen for 'Our School' and 'Growing Up'; Doubleday, a division of Bantam, Doubleday Publishing, Doubleday Publishing Group, Inc. for 'The Tom Cat' by Don Marquis © 1917 Sun Printing and Publishing Association, from *Poems and Portraits*; Romanus Egudu and Donatus Nwoga (editors) for 'You!' from *Igbo Traditional Verse*; Jimi Rand for 'Black Man's Song'; Penguin Books Ltd for 'Bad Dog' and 'Rain' from *Late Home* by Brian Lee (pages 11,12) © Brian Lee 1976 and 'Teachers – the Inside Story' ('Rodge Said') by Michael Rosen from *You Tell Me* by Roger McGough and Michael Rosen (Kestrel Books) © Michael Rosen, 1979; John Kitching for 'My Gerbil' and 'Why?'; Oxford University Press for 'Execution' by Gregory Harrison © Gregory Harrison 1982, reprinted from *Catch the Light: Poems by Laurence Smith, Gregory Harrison and Vernon Scannell* 1982; Pam Ayres for 'Please Will You Take Your Children Home Before I Do Them In' © Pam Ayres; Vernon Scannell for 'Intelligence Test' and 'The Apple Raid'; Brian Patten for 'The School Caretaker', 'Someone Stole the – ' and 'Gust Becos I Cud Not Spel' from *Gargling with Jelly* © Brian Patten 1985 reproduced by permission of Penguin Books Ltd; Grace Nicholls and Virago Press for 'Two Old Blackmen on a Leicester Square Bench'; John Agard for 'Palm Tree King'; Geoffrey Summerfield for 'Lurker' and 'Ess'ole' from *Welcome and Other Poems* published by André Deutsch Ltd; Joan M Batchelor for 'My Birthday Treat'; Jack Prelutsky and A. and C. Black (Publishers) Ltd for 'The Vampire' from *Nightmares: Poems to Trouble Your Sleep*; Mike Starkey and Kingsway Publications for 'At First it Didn't Matter' from *Frogs and Princes* by Mike Starkey; Charles Causley for 'Colonel Fazackerley' and 'Angel Hill' from *Figgie Hobbin* by Charles Causley published by Macmillan; Roger McGough for 'Sky in the Pie' from *Sky in the Pie* published by Kestrel Books Ltd, reprinted by permission of A. D. Peters and Co Ltd; Spike Milligan for 'Veggy Lion' from *Unspun Socks from a Chicken's Laundry* published by Michael Joseph; Richard Rieu for 'Portrait of a House' and 'The Paint Box' by E. V. Rieu; Colin West for 'Socks' from *It's Funny When You Look At It* by Colin West published by Century Hutchinson Publishing Group Ltd; Trevor Millum for 'Swap? Sell? Small Ads Sell Fast'; Edwin Morgan and the Carcanet Press Ltd for 'The Computer's First Christmas Card' from *Poems of 30 years* by Edwin Morgan; May Swenson for 'Southbound on the Freeway', first published in *The New Yorker* © 1963 May Swenson; Daphne Schiller for 'I Had Rather Be a Woman'; The Literary Trustees of Walter de la Mare and the Society of Authors as their representative for 'Snow' by Walter de la Mare; Michael Rosen for 'The Longest Journey in the World' from *You Can't Catch Me* published by André Deutsch Ltd.